The IEA Health and Welfare Unit

Choice in Welfare No. 41

Benefit Dependency:
How Welfare Undermines Independence

David G. Green

nit

First published January 1998
2nd Impression with minor corrections, January 1999

The IEA Health and Welfare Unit
2 Lord North St
London SW1P 3LB

ISBN 0-255 36433-4
ISSN 1362-9565

Typeset by the IEA Health and Welfare Unit
in Bookman 10 point
Printed in Great Britain by
St Edmundsbury Press Ltd
Blenheim Industrial Park, Newmarket Road
Bury St Edmunds, Suffolk

Contents

The Author

David G. Green is the Director of the Health and Welfare Unit at the Institute of Economic Affairs. He was formerly a Labour councillor in Newcastle upon Tyne from 1976 until 1981, and from 1981 to 1983 was a Research Fellow at the Australian National University in Canberra.

His books include *Power and Party in an English City*, Allen & Unwin, 1980; *Mutual Aid or Welfare State*, Allen & Unwin, 1984 (with L. Cromwell); *Working Class Patients and the Medical Establishment*, Temple Smith/Gower, 1985; and *The New Right: The Counter Revolution in Political, Economic and Social Thought*, Wheatsheaf, 1987. His work has also been published in journals such as *The Journal of Social Policy*, *Political Quarterly*, *Philosophy of the Social Sciences*, and *Policy and Politics*. He wrote the chapter on 'The Neo-Liberal Perspective' in *The Student's Companion to Social Policy*, Blackwell, 1998.

The IEA has published his *The Welfare State: For Rich or for Poor?*, 1982; *Which Doctor?*, 1985; *Challenge to the NHS*, 1986; *Medicines in the Marketplace*, 1987; *Everyone a Private Patient*, 1988; *Should Doctors Advertise?*, 1989; *Equalizing People*, 1990; *Medicard: A Better Way to Pay for Medicines?*, 1993 (with David Lucas); *Reinventing Civil Society*, 1993; and *Community Without Politics*, 1996.

Acknowledgements

Special thanks go to Norman Dennis, Peter Saunders and Robert Whelan for comments on early drafts. I am also grateful to Barry Macleod-Cullinane for research assistance.

It goes without saying that they are not to blame for remaining errors in the finished product.

Preface

The Blair Government's declared strategy for reforming welfare represents a sharp break with the recent past. In his speech to the Labour Party's 1997 conference Tony Blair went so far as to say that 'a decent society is *not* based on rights'. It is based on our duty to each other. The new welfare system 'must encourage work, not dependency'. The long-term unemployed and the young were to benefit from a £3.5 billion investment in work and training but they would be compelled to take one of the options on offer. Single mothers with school-age children must at least visit a job centre and 'not just stay at home waiting for the benefit cheque every week until the children are 16'.

These were strong words signifying a real change of strategy. The intention of this publication is to launch a new series of figures—the Independence Figures—to monitor the Government's success in reducing welfare dependency. The first issue of the Independence Figures shows how dependency has grown during the course of this century. Future publications will reveal whether public policies have succeeded or failed in restoring the independence and strength of character that has been the historical norm in Britain.

In addition, *Benefit Dependency: How Welfare Undermines Independence* examines the arguments of Tony Blair's old-Labour critics typified by the 50 or so professors of sociology and social policy who wrote to the *Financial Times* in October 1997 regretting New Labour's abandonment of policies intended to redistribute income and wealth. As they rightly inferred, their doctrine of equalisation is not compatible with the ideal of a society built on duty to each other.

David G. Green

Introduction

In recent years, there has been a huge increase in the number of people who look to politicians for the means of life. In 1951 about four per cent of the population relied on the chief means-tested benefit, national assistance. Today nearly 17 per cent rely on its successor, income support. This figure does not include reliance on housing benefit, council tax benefit, national insurance benefits, like unemployment benefit (now jobseeker's allowance); universal benefits, such as child benefit; and 'fringe' benefits like mortgage interest relief. If the other main means-tested benefits (housing benefit and council tax benefit) are included the figure is 27 per cent. Reliance on benefits began to grow steadily from the 1960s and has accelerated in the 1980s and 1990s.

Looked at the other way round, during the first half of this century about 95 per cent or more of the population were usually independent of state support. By 1961 about 95 per cent remained independent and as late as 1971 over 91 per cent. Today, the figure is only 83 per cent.

This represents a vast increase in dependence on the state. We can compare the numbers reliant on income support or its equivalent back to the nineteenth century. Reliable figures are available from 1871, but there are estimates before that. For instance, when Tocqueville visited England in 1833, he estimated that 16-17 per cent (one-sixth) of the population were reliant on poor relief.[1] By 1871 the proportion of the population of England and Wales receiving poor relief had been reduced to under five per cent. By 1901 the figure had fallen to 2.5 per cent[2] and was not to change significantly until the 1960s. In 1931 the figure was still about 2.5 per cent, and by 1951, four per cent relied on national assistance, as it was then called. In 1961 the figure was still only 5.1 per cent. There was then a significant increase to 8.4 per cent by 1971, but the proportion was still comparable to the historical norm.

Does it matter? Some commentators remain unconcerned about the proportion of the population reliant on the state. They focus only on the cash value of benefits, which they find too low. A recent report published by the Joseph Rowntree Foundation, for instance, argued that increasing benefits by about £15 a week would solve a great many problems.[3]

There is a counter view. It is that if too many people look to the government for the means of life, then this dependency has harmful effects which accumulate over time. The initial harm results from people organising their affairs so that they qualify for benefit. Having crossed the boundary between independent self-support and reliance on the work of others, individuals are inclined to neglect friendships or relationships with people who could provide a helping hand in a spirit of mutual respect. Because their self-respect diminishes, they often become more shameless in their determination to live at the expense of others. They also fail to join organisations like churches or voluntary associations, where they would meet people who would gladly provide temporary, restorative help. As a further consequence, they acquire fewer skills of co-operating with others, and face fewer challenges. In turn, they have fewer opportunities to strengthen their characters by overcoming adversity. As a result, they are more prone to manipulation by politicians, some of whom are only too willing to 'buy' their votes with promises of 'more'. Politicians whose model of society is one of leaders and led are very happy to preserve in being a section of the population that will trade its votes for cash rewards.

Worse still, such dependency on the state tends to undermine the public spirit, personal responsibility and commitment to serve others that make a free society possible. It encourages a view of the political process, not as the domain of legitimate action in common, but as a means of gaining advantage at the expense of others.

The impact on the social security budget in Great Britain has been huge. Between 1981/82 and 1995/96 there was an increase in real terms of 62 per cent.[4] Expenditure due to unemployment increased by 21 per cent from £7.5 billion in 1981/82 to £9.0 billion in 1995/96, but social security spending due to family breakdown rose from £2.1 billion to £9.5 billion, a 345 per cent increase. Expenditure on the elderly increased by 36 per cent, an increase that seems modest compared with that for long-term sickness and disability, which increased by 257 per cent to £21.2 billion.[5] In 1996/97 the cost of benefits for the sick and disabled (£23 billion) exceeded the total cost of the army, navy and air force put together.

There are three rival views today about the purpose of a social security system: the 'relief', 'equalisation' and 'independence' traditions.

The 'relief' tradition aims to relieve the hardship of the poor by providing cash support. Two distinct traditions of thought sustain it: sympathy for the poor, stemming especially from religious sentiment; and a pragmatic desire to 'buy-off' discontented groups.

Supporters of 'equalisation' focus on the 'economic distance' between sections of the population. As a doctrine it is inseparable from the ideal of a society that puts leaders in charge and expects little of the masses. The leaders defend their power as necessary to advance the interests of the led, who are to benefit from income transfers.

The 'independence' tradition aspires to encourage everyone to be self-supporting and therefore as capable of making an independent contribution to the good of all as possible. It goes hand in hand with the ideal of a free society built on the good character of its members.

The 'relief' approach has been predominant among Conservatives and the 'equalisation' approach has traditionally been the preserve of socialists. Among intellectuals who identify themselves with the left, equalisation is still the predominant view. In October 1997 some fifty professors of social policy and sociology wrote to the *Financial Times*[6] to complain that the Blair government had abandoned redistribution as an objective. The government's stance, however, reflects the return of many socialists to the 'independence' view, which was central to the 'ethical socialist' standpoint. Typically, they argue that social security should be a 'springboard'. Labour's Social Justice Commission[7] and Frank Field[8] have led the way. Many Conservatives are moving in the same direction, but opinions are divided. While in office, Kenneth Clarke, for instance, favoured the 'pragmatic relief' approach (if benefits are not generous there will be street riots) and Peter Lilley, as Secretary of State for Social Security, favoured the encouragement of independence through schemes such as the jobseeker's allowance.

Behind these contradictory combinations within political movements lie the two intellectual traditions that have been at the heart of British political discourse in recent centuries: 'liberty' and 'collectivism'. Neither has been uniquely the property of any one political party and today all the main political parties draw upon elements from each.

The tradition of 'collectivism' puts its faith in the capacity of leaders and has little confidence in the qualities of the rank and file. Its favourite analogy is the team under leadership.

Collectivism is based on a view of the human condition that explains behaviour as the result of forces beyond individual control. Most people are held not to be in command of their fate, a view sustained by two powerful intellectual currents for much of the twentieth century. Marxism held that forces outside the individual dictated events (the economic structure) whereas Freudianism emphasised *inner* forces that impelled people irrationally to behave in particular ways. Both theories assumed, even if their protagonists did not always say so, that the leaders were immune from the forces that moulded others. Sometimes this division into 'sophisticated' leaders and the 'helpless' mass led to tyranny, but in the West it led to paternalistic-but-democratic government, whose task was to use the political system to serve the interests of a section of the population — the working class or the poor.

Marxism is no longer taken seriously, but the tradition of paternalistic government remains with us. Partly because they see themselves as leaders of the majority, and partly because of the electoral imperative that a majority of votes must be won, paternalistic leaders are inclined to adopt a wide definition of the 'poor' or 'deprived' who are to benefit from political action. This tendency is one of the main causes of the 'poverty inflation' described in Chapter 2.

The counter view — liberty under law — had fallen out of favour by the early part of the 20th century. It assumed that all are capable of independent judgement and that the purpose of life is the rational pursuit of ideals or aims, preferably by individuals applying themselves to improvement of social conditions in whatever way they believe best. Adam Smith, J.S. Mill and Kant were leading exponents. It rested on the ideal of the self-improving individual, capable of self-support, serving others and upholding the shared institutions of civil society as a personal obligation. Believers in liberty, like believers in 'relief', were naturally concerned for the well being of individuals who looked to the government to require other people to support them rather than to their own efforts—not out of any lack of sympathy, but because they were not participating to the full in their birthright of liberty.

Liberty 'rightly understood' does not hold that the basic building block of capitalism is the self-interested individual; rather, it maintains that the fundamental building block of a society is the self-improving character. The institutions of a free society—not least the law, marriage and the family—are structures necessary to sustain and encourage a society of independent-but-united, self-improving but not self-serving individuals. The ideal is of strong characters who are capable, when circumstances require it, of standing apart from the crowd on matters of principle, and yet prepared when necessary to sacrifice their own interests for the good of others and to play their part in upholding the *mores*, morals and institutions that persist—indeed can only survive—so long as they are supported by the daily actions of each person going about his or her ordinary affairs.

A public policy to assist the poor, according to this tradition, should not be content with handing over cash but rather seek to discover why an individual is not independent. Paternalists sometimes claim that no one is truly 'independent', by which they mean 'isolated'. But the independence valued in the liberal tradition is not 'isolation'; it is the capacity to serve others and, at the very minimum, the capacity to be self-supporting and thus not an avoidable burden on other people.

To sum up: the great divide in social policy is between, on the one hand, those (collectivists) who have little confidence in the capacities of the rank and file and much confidence in the capacity of leaders; and, on the other, the champions of liberty, with their high expectations of human potential under the guidance of wise institutions rather than under the leadership of politicians.

The rest of this essay is organised as follows.

Chapter 1 shows how dependence on the state has increased and how independence has correspondingly diminished.

Chapter 2 discusses the focus of the poverty lobby, whose concern has been to define and measure poverty in order to give the impression that the poor are getting poorer and that more people are falling below the poverty line. Chapter 2 argues that the guiding philosophy of the poverty lobbyists, who exaggerate the extent of poverty, has been 'equalisation' rather than independence.

Chapter 3 deals with the 'independence' tradition of welfare, describing its historical roots and modern relevance. It is different in style from Chapter 2, which is inevitably somewhat technical. In reality, however, few poverty lobbyists hold their views on technical grounds. Their true motivation is rooted in egalitarian sentiment and doubts about the moral credentials of the 'independence' tradition. For this reason I have devoted Chapter 3 to an explanation of the aims and rationale of the latter tradition. Particular attention is devoted to the term 'character', which fell out of favour, especially after the Second World War. More recently, it has been rehabilitated, not least because, with characteristic courage, Frank Field in *Making Welfare Work* and Norman Dennis in *English Ethical Socialism* have reminded the intellectual left of its place in earlier Labour thought. As a result, in his first speech as prime minister to a Labour Party conference Tony Blair spoke of a new Britain, 'Held together by our values and by the strength of our character'.

There are many on the left of politics who wish to be champions of the poor, but who have been misled into believing that egalitarianism is the best political strategy. Chapter 3 argues that sympathy for the less-fortunate need not entail egalitarianism.

The study recommends that the Government's Households Below Average Income (HBAI) series should be scrapped and replaced by a series of Independence Figures that highlights the success or failure of public policies in encouraging independence.

1

Dependence and Independence: the Trends

This chapter charts the trend in falling independence. The intention over the next few years is to publish the figures annually and gradually to refine the method of calculation. For the present the narrowest definition of dependence has been used. With luck, regular publication will encourage public debate about the best methods of encouraging independence and lead to a change in the direction of the trend lines. Instead of putting out press releases expressing pride in having increased the 'take-up' rate of benefits, perhaps public policy makers will take satisfaction from increasing independence.

The Independence Figures

According to the Royal Commission on the Poor Laws of 1909[1] reliable information is only available from 1871 and Table 1 (p. 3) shows figures from that date until 1931. Table 2 (p. 4) shows the figures after the 1948 national insurance scheme came into effect. After that date the figures distinguish between claimants and their dependants. Before that dependants were included, but because the figures are not strictly comparable they are shown in a separate table.

There are other complications in making comparisons over such a long period. After 1908, reliance on the poor law does not fully reflect dependence on state benefits. In that year, non-contributory pensions were introduced, soon to be followed by a stream of other benefits which increased the methods by which a person could become reliant on the state. According to Beveridge, in 1901 in England and Wales one in 16 of the population were men over 65 or women over 60, while in 1941 it was one in eight. About half the pauperism in 1906 was due to old age and nearly one in three of the over-70s relied on the poor law.[2] By 1909 about 500,000 people were in receipt of pensions under the 1908 Act, many of whom might otherwise have come to rely on poor relief.

Other legislation also introduced new state benefits. The 1911 National Insurance Act introduced sick pay and, under Part II, unemployment insurance for 2.25 million employees. Unemployment benefit was extended in 1916 to another 1.5 million, and the Unemployment Insurance Act of 1920 extended it to 11 million people altogether.[3]

Unemployment insurance was never established on actuarially sound principles. Even before the 1920 Act came into effect in 1921, adjustments had to be made which undermined the insurance principle. In fact, the inconsistency had set in earlier with the military out-of-work donation, introduced in 1918 for servicemen who did not have a job after demobilisation. It was followed by an extended benefit scheme for those who had not worked long enough to qualify for unemployment benefit. In effect, by 1921 the principle of benefit 'as of right', regardless of insurance contributions, had been established. In 1927 transitional benefit was introduced, initially as a temporary measure to be cancelled in 1929, but it was extended until the establishment of the Unemployment Assistance Board in 1934.

The Unemployment Assistance Board took responsibility for the unemployed who did not qualify for insurance from January 1935 and relaxed conditions still further. In 1937 a further 100,000 persons, previously the responsibility of the public assistance committees, were taken on by the Unemployment Assistance Board. (In 1929 the poor law guardians had been abolished and local authorities had been required to establish public assistance committees to assume their responsibilities.)

Further relaxation followed in 1941. Until that year public assistance for the able-bodied unemployed not entitled to insurance was subject to a means test that took into account the resources of the whole household. However, the Determination of Needs Act, 1941, replaced it with a personal means test which took no account of the resources of other household members.

In 1925 the Widows', Orphans', and Old Age Contributory Pensions Act had been introduced, the first national scheme of contributory pensions (the 1908 scheme was means-tested and financed from general taxes). The benefits had come into force in three stages. From January 1926, there were pensions of 10s (50p) a week for widows. From July 1926, old age pensions at 10s a week were granted without a means test to persons then over the age of 70. And from January 1928, pensions of 10s a week were paid to insured persons already aged between 65 and 70; and henceforward to all insured men reaching the age of 65, as well as their wives.

The 1940 Old Age and Widows' Pensions Act provided that, from July 1940, the old age pension of 10s a week should be payable from the age of 60, instead of 65, to an insured woman or the wife of an insured man who had attained the age of 65. This Act also introduced supplementary pensions for needy old-age pensioners and widow pensioners over the age of 60. The responsibility for supplementary pensions was placed on the Unemployment Assistance Board, which was renamed the Assistance Board.[4]

Thus, from 1908, dependency on the poor law does not fully reflect dependency on the state. However, the figures in Tables 1 and 2 are for the poor law and its successors only: poor relief until 1929, public assistance until 1948, national assistance until 1966, supplementary benefit until 1988, and subsequently income support. Nor do Tables 1 and 2 take into account partial dependence. The bias of this method is to under-state reliance on government benefits.

Table 1
Dependence on Poor Relief, England and Wales, 1871-1931

Year	Benefit Recipients	Dependants	Total	% of population
1871	-	-	1,037,360	4.6
1901	-	-	705,183	2.5
1921	-	-	1,366,569	3.6
1931	-	-	969,533	2.4

Sources: The figures for 1871 and 1901 are from the Annual Reports of the Local Government Board. They are for England and Wales and show all recipients of poor relief on 1 January in each year.[5]

The figure for 1921 is for England and Wales and is taken from Ministry of Health, Annual Report.[6] It shows recipients of poor relief at the end of December, including dependants. The 1931 figure is from Ministry of Health, Annual Report.[7] It is an average figure for the whole year, including all recipients of domestic and domiciliary relief. Dependants of recipients of domiciliary relief are included.

Table 2
Dependence on
National Assistance/Supplementary Benefit/Income Support,
Great Britain, 1951-1996

Year	Benefit Recipients	Dependants	Total	% of population	GDP Index
1951	1,461,626	608,000	2,069,626	4.2	37.6
1961	1,844,000	764,000	2,608,000	5.1	49.3
1971	2,909,000	1,655,000	4,564,000	8.4	65.3
1981	3,723,000	2,398,000	6,121,000	11.2	76.0
1991	4,487,000	3,260,000	7,747,000	13.8	97.9
1992	5,088,000	3,765,000	8,853,000	15.7	97.4
1993	5,643,000	4,180,000	9,822,000	17.4	99.6
1994	5,675,000	4,177,000	9,852,000	17.4	103.5
1995	5,670,000	4,103,000	9,773,000	17.2	106.2
1996	5,549,000	4,038,000	9,587,000	16.8	-

Sources: The National Assistance Board was responsible for means-tested benefits from 1948. The figures for 1951 and 1961 are for Great Britain, and record the number of individuals and their dependants receiving weekly allowances at the end of December each year.[8]

The 1971 figures are from the *Annual Report of the Department of Health and Social Security*.[9] The calculation is based on the number receiving weekly allowances and their dependants in November 1971.

The figures for 1981 are from *Social Security Statistics, 1982*.[10] They show recipients of regular supplementary benefit payments and their dependants in November/December in Great Britain.[11]

Figures for 1991-1996 are from *Social Security Statistics, 1997*. Figures for 1991 and subsequently show recipients in May, when there are usually fewer claimants than in the winter months for which earlier figures are reported.[12] They can be compared with figures from the *Households Below Average Income* report which compared administrative data with Family Expenditure Survey (FES) findings.[13]

The population figures are from the *Annual Abstract of Statistics* for various years. ONS mid-year estimates are used for later years.

GDP is from *Social Trends, 1997*, Table 5.28. The table shows GDP for the United Kingdom at factor cost. This measure of GDP excludes taxes on expenditure and subsidies. Index: 1990=100.

Figure 1 (p. 9) shows the same information as a graph. It particularly highlights the scale of the change in the last 20 years.

How can this growth in dependency be explained? First, it is not because of falling prosperity. As the sixth column in Table 2 shows, GDP since 1951 has been rising steadily. To answer this question Table 3 shows how the recipients of income support and its predecessors have changed over the years. Figure 2 (p. 9) shows the same data as a graph.

Table 3
National Assistance, Supplementary Benefit and Income Support by Type of Recipient, 1951-1995

Thousands

	1951	1961	1971	1981	1991	1992	1993	1994	1995	1996
Total	1,462	1,844	2,909	3,720	4,487	5,088	5,643	5,765	5,670	5,549
Pensioners	891	1,154	1,919	1,740	1,575	1,643	1,736	1,765	1,781	1,764
Sick and Disabled	121	134	305	221	375	425	527	618	739	786
Unemployed	364	479	387	1,318	1,335	1,662	1,920	1,828	1,672	1,495
Widows	86	77	65	16	4	4	4	4	-	-
One-parent Families	89	97	213	369	871	957	1,013	1,039	1,056	1,059
Misc	-	-	20	61	331	401	446	425	422	444

Notes: This table shows the recipients of benefit and not their dependants. Figures for 1951 and 1961 from National Assistance Board, Annual Report, 1961, p. 51; 1971 from DHSS, Annual Report, p. 334. 1981 from *Social Security Statistics*, 1982, p. 186; 1991 from *Social Security Statistics*, 1992, p. 20; 1992-1995, from *Social Security Statistics*, 1996; 1996 figures from *Social Security Statistics*, 1997. The number of widows for 1991-1994 is from *Social Security Statistics*, 1996, p. 24.

One-parent families for 1951 from National Assistance Board, Annual Report, p. 6. There were 38,000 separated or deserted wives and 51,000 others, described as 'mostly women with domestic ties, usually children'. From this description not all were women with children and some would have been caring for other relatives, but I have included all 51,000 in the calculation. One-parent families for 1961 are from National Assistance Board, Annual Report, pp. 12-13. There were 76,000 separated or divorced wives under 60 and 21,000 'unmarried mothers'.

Unemployment has played a varying part and remains significant at 29 per cent of the total, but the biggest change has been the reduced dependency of pensioners on benefits. In 1951 pensioners made up over 60 per cent of National Assistance recipients, but by 1995 they comprised 31 per cent.

Sickness and disability accounted for 8.2 per cent in 1951, increasing to 13 per cent by 1995, but the breakdown of the family is currently the biggest single driver of growing dependency.

In 1951 89,000 claimants were described as unmarried mothers, separated, divorced or deserted wives, some 6 per cent of claimants. By 1991 there were 1,056,000 one-parent families claiming income support, 18 per cent of the total.

It is sometimes argued that unemployment is one of the causes of family breakdown, but a comparison of the trends in Figure 3 (p. 10) contradicts this claim. Unemployment fluctuates over the period, whereas family breakdown increases remarkably steadily regardless of the variations in unemployment. This conclusion holds whether family breakdown is measured by the reliance of one-parent families on benefits or using the official estimates of all one-parent families, available only from 1971.

The financial significance of family breakdown is illustrated by Figure 4 (p. 11) which compares benefit expenditure due to unemployment with that for the one-parent family. In 1995/96, for the first time, the cost of family breakdown to the social security budget exceeded the cost of unemployment.

Tables 1 and 2 show only the recipients of the main means-tested benefit and many such recipients are unemployed. But in addition there are further unemployed people receiving unemployment benefit (now jobseeker's allowance). Tables 4 and 5 show the total number of recipients of unemployment benefit and the main means-tested benefit.

Table 4 shows a time series from 1921 to 1935 to allow a comparison between today's situation and the worst years of the Depression. The figure for poor relief in Great Britain includes dependants, whereas the unemployment benefit figure does not. For simplicity I have compared total recipients of poor relief (including dependants) and unemployment benefit to the total population of Great Britain.

Table 5 covers 1951-1996, but after 1948 it is possible to distinguish between recipients of benefit and their dependants. It would be preferable to express the number as a percentage of the total population excluding children, but to facilitate comparison with the 1920s and 1930s claimants are compared with the total population of Great Britain. The effect is to inflate the proportion of the population in the 1920s and 1930s relying on

poor relief and unemployment benefit, to the extent that dependants are included in the poor relief figure. Despite this bias, the
worst figure for the 1930s was exceeded in the early 1990s. The
result is the same if an estimate of dependants is added to the
number of recipients of unemployment benefit in the 1930s, but
I have used the more-reliable claimant count to make the
comparison.

Table 4
Poor Relief and the Insured Unemployed, 1921-1935

Thousands

Year	Poor relief	Insured Unemployed	Total	% of GB population
1921	754	1,594	2,348	5.5
1926	1,679	1,318	2,997	6.8
1931	1,319	2,663	3,982	8.9
1932	1,485	2,855	4,340	9.6
1933	1,789	2,955	4,744	10.5
1934	1,843	2,407	4,250	9.4
1935	2,013	2,333	4,346	9.5

Conclusion

Perhaps the simplest way to look at the trend since the last war
is to look at the falling proportion of the population that has been
independent of the main means-tested benefit (national assistance, supplementary benefit or income support). The results are
shown in Table 6.

Table 5
National Assistance, Supplementary Benefit, Income Support and Unemployment Benefit Recipients, 1951-1996

Thousands

Year	NA/SB/IS Recipients	UB Only	Total	% GB population
1951	1,462	202	1,664	3.4
1961	1,844	174	2,018	3.9
1971	2,909	302	3,211	5.9
1981	3,723	940	4,663	8.5
1991	4,487	453	4,940	8.8
1992	5,088	545	5,633	10.0
1993	5,643	543	6,186	10.9
1994	5,675	428	6,103	10.8
1995	5,670	283	5,953	10.5
1996	5,549	341	5,890	10.3

Sources: 1991 from *Social Security Statistics*, 1996, p. 128; 1992-1996 from *Social Security Statistics*, 1997, p. 128. Earlier years from Field, F., *Making Welfare Work*, p. 148.

Table 6
The Independence Figures 1951 - 1996

Year	Recipients of National Assistance/ Supplementary Benefit/ Income Support and their dependants	% of population remaining independent
1951	2,069,626	95.8
1961	2,608,000	94.9
1971	4,564,000	91.6
1981	6,121,000	88.8
1991	7,747,000	86.2
1992	8,853,000	84.3
1993	9,822,000	82.6
1994	9,852,000	82.6
1995	9,773,000	82.8
1996	9,587,000	83.2

Source: See Table 2.

Figure 1
Dependence, 1871- 1996

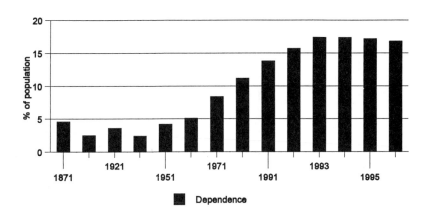

Figure 2
Income Support by Main Types of Recipient, Percentages 1951-1996

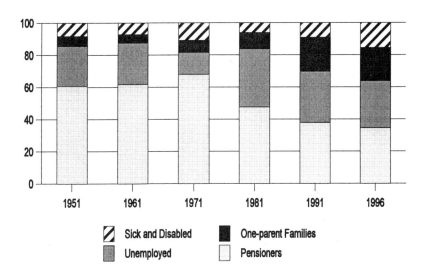

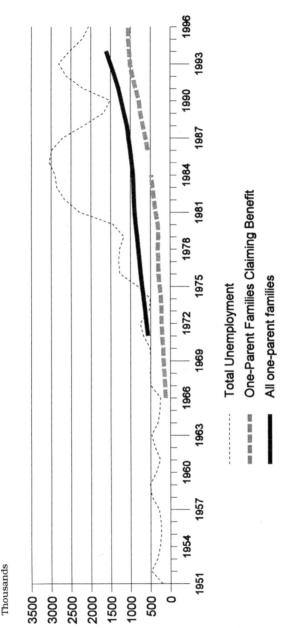

Figure 3
Unemployment and One-Parent Families 1951-1996

Thousands

Total Unemployment

One-Parent Families Claiming Benefit

All one-parent families

Sources: Unemployment figures from the Annual Abstract of Statistics for various years. Figures are for June in each year. One-parent family estimate from Haskey, J., 'Estimated numbers of one-parent families and their prevalence in Great Britain in 1991', *Population Trends*, no. 78, Winter 1994, pp. 5-19. Figures for 1993 and 1994 estimated from Haskey, IEA, forthcoming. One-parent families receiving benefit, see notes to Table 3. No official figure given for 1985.

Figure 4
Benefit Expenditure 1981/82 - 1996/97

£000m

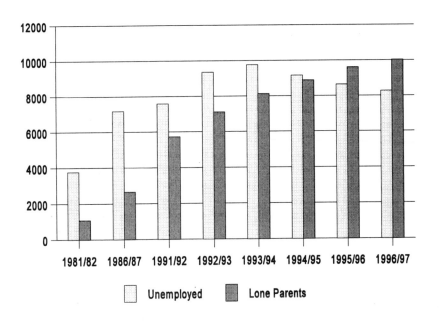

Source: *Social Security Statistics*, 1996 ; from 1992/93-1996/97, *Social Security Statistics*, 1997, p. 3.

2

Poverty Inflation

Typical headline claims in recent years include: 'the poor got poorer'; more people are 'in poverty'; and 'trickle-down' is not working. What is the basis of these claims?

There are two sets of issues. First, how poverty is defined; and second how it is studied and measured. On both counts, the typical claims of the poverty lobby are open to criticism.

Definition of the Poverty Line

The manner in which a writer defines poverty reflects his underlying assumptions about the human condition and his preferred role for government.

If the paramount purpose is to uphold a society in which as many people as possible can be independent, then the focus will be on the number of individuals relying on the state and the objective of policy will be to keep the number as low as possible — not for the sake of reducing taxes, but because the quality of life without independence is much impaired. Behind this view lies a conception of the ideal life, to be described more fully in Chapter 3, which is not defined by material consumption but by the personal qualities of each person. To strive to be materially self-sufficient is to fulfil the minimum obligation we owe to one another, namely not needlessly to rely on other people. More positively, it is to equip oneself to be of service.

To focus on relative income or relative deprivation, in the manner of the typical modern poverty study, suggests a desire to define as many people as possible as poor in the hope of stimulating political action on their behalf. The underlying assumption is of an inert group requiring the delivery of benefits by the political system. Moreover, the 'relative' approach is not built on respect for the actual or potential independence of the poor. The aim of policy is not to empower them to make contributions to the good of all, but to give them cash. The practical result, to be explained more fully below, has been to diminish the personal qualities of welfare recipients, thus reducing their capacity to contribute to the common good. Relative definitions suggest an ambition to impose egalitarian policies. The assumption is of powerless people who are excluded—with 'no stake in society' —who can, however, be 'included' by means of cash transfers.[1]

In *The Invention of Permanent Poverty* Norman Dennis describes the process of 'poverty inflation' which, by re-defining poverty, allowed an ever-increasing number of people to be identified as the class requiring political action on their behalf. Over the years the line was raised to catch ever more people. In the early 1960s the poverty line was the national assistance (later supplementary benefit and income support) level. Then it was the state minimum plus 40 per cent, allowing writers to speak of people in poverty and 'on the margins of poverty'. Subsequently, the poverty line was a percentage of average or median income, and then it became 'exclusion' from the dominant lifestyle. At each step the intention was to exploit the sympathy that the term 'poverty' evokes.[2]

By the time Peter Townsend, the doyen of poverty researchers, produced his landmark *Poverty in the United Kingdom* in 1979,[3] he found that three measures of poverty were in use: the state-benefit standard; relative income; and relative deprivation.

By the state-benefit standard Townsend meant the supplementary benefit level, now called income support.

The 'relative income' standard usually relies on defining the 'middle' income and asking how many people are below some percentage of it. Typically an individual's or a household's income is compared with a benchmark representing the mid-point, such as the median or the average income. The Government's Households Below Average Income series uses this method and goes on to divide the population into income deciles or quintiles and to compare the differences between them. The ruling idea is that the 'economic distance' between members of a society is important.

According to Townsend, there are two weaknesses in the concept of relative income. First, income varies with household size and so it is difficult to decide on the unit to study (individuals, families or households). Second, any benchmark is bound to be somewhat arbitrary. If 50 per cent of the average is chosen, then why not 40 per cent or 80 per cent?[4] His relative-deprivation standard tried to overcome the arbitrariness of measures like '50 per cent of the average' by defining the community 'style of living' as the poverty line. At various incomes, says Townsend, people 'drop out or are excluded' from this style of living.[5] To establish his line, he developed sixty indicators, including diet, clothing and holidays.[6]

This method of defining a 'dominant lifestyle' allows the poverty line to be drawn substantially above the cash amount necessary for physical efficiency and well above the state safety net, thus enabling Townsend to declare that 25 per cent of households (or 23 per cent of individuals—12,460,000) were 'in poverty' in 1968/69, the period to which his study relates.[7]

According to the state-benefit standard (the basic supplementary benefit scales plus housing costs), only seven per cent of households were 'in poverty' (six per cent of individuals). On the relative income standard (households having an income of less than 50 per cent of the mean for their type), 10.5 per cent of households and nine per cent of individuals (5 million) were in poverty.[8]

Relative definitions, which link the poverty line to the average or median during a period of rising prosperity, have proved to be effective, if not infallible, methods for declaring a large proportion of the population to be perpetually 'poor'. Consequently critics of relative definitions often argue for an absolute line so that progress over time can be measured. Rowntree's studies of York between 1901 and 1951 provide an example of an attempt to maintain a comparison against a 'poverty line' over a long period. Rowntree's poverty line had to be re-adjusted over the years as lifestyles changed but it did represent a reasonably stable benchmark.[9] His approach was to define the minimum 'basket of goods' necessary to sustain life and to discover how many people fell below that line. Rowntree's minimum-basket-of-goods approach had fallen out of favour by the mid-1960s, though it still has adherents today, not least Professor Jonathan Bradshaw of York University.

The US poverty line is also based on a minimum. The official poverty line defines a person or family as poor if the cost of a stipulated package of food is more than one-third of their income.

Some poverty lobbyists, such as Townsend, argue that 'absolute poverty' disintegrates on close inspection because apparently objective needs are in reality 'socially determined'.[10] Professor Tony Atkinson, in making the same point, gives the example of taking a bath. To obtain a job today, it would usually be an advantage to look clean, for which a bath or shower is necessary, whereas similar cleanliness was not essential during the nineteenth century.[11]

But, because lifestyles change over time, it does not follow that any fixed definition of sufficiency over the short run is useless. Moreover, it does not follow from the statement that minimum acceptable standards are 'socially determined' and vary over the years that a relative definition is always preferable. A definition of poverty based on the 'acceptable minimum' can serve a useful purpose, not only over a relatively short period of 10-15 years, but also as a means of permitting comparisons between generations. As Dennis has shown, a principal concern of poverty researchers until the early 1960s was to establish whether children were better off or worse off than their parents and grandparents.[12] Relative definitions obliterate any such comparison.

The real significance of a writer like Townsend is that he has a wider agenda: to reduce the power of the rich. He says, for example, that: 'To comprehend and explain poverty is also to comprehend and explain riches'.[13] The theoretical approach of his book, he says, is 'rooted in class relations'.[14] And his 'chief conclusion' is that:

> poverty is more extensive than is generally or officially believed and has to be understood not only as an inevitable feature of severe social inequality but also as a particular consequence of actions by the rich to preserve and enhance their wealth and so deny it to others. Control of wealth and of the institutions created by that wealth, and therefore of the terms under which it may be generated and passed on selectively or for the general good, is therefore central to any policies designed to abolish or alleviate the condition.[15]

His policy recommendations reveal a willingness to impose extensive controls over individual lives. An 'effective assault' on poverty should include:

- Abolition of excessive wealth. The wealth of the rich must be substantially reduced by a variety of policies including the imposition of a statutory definition of maximum permissible wealth in relation to the mean.

- Abolition of excessive income. Top salaries or wages must be substantially reduced in relation to the mean and a statutory definition of maximum permissible earnings (and income) agreed.

- Introduction of an equitable income structure and some breaking down of the distinction between earners and dependants. At the logical extreme this might involve the withdrawal of personal income taxation and of the social security benefits scheme, and the payment of tax-free incomes according to a publicly agreed and controlled schedule by occupational category and skill, but also by need or dependency.[16]

Today's enthusiasts for relative definitions of poverty may not share Townsend's ultimate objectives but their work, consciously or unconsciously, rests on similar egalitarian assumptions.

Measurement of the Standard of Living

I turn now to a more technical question: what is the best method of discovering the standard of life being lived? There is one preliminary issue. The chief source for modern poverty statistics is the Family Expenditure Survey (FES). It is the source for the government's main series of poverty statistics, *Households Below Average Income* (HBAI).

I will focus on the Rowntree Inquiry of 1995. The criticisms could be directed against the HBAI method introduced by the Conservatives after they abandoned the *Low Income Families* series based on benefit dependency, but the Rowntree Inquiry is significant because it gave added credibility to factual claims about poverty that are open to serious challenge. It did so because its membership included an apparent cross-section of society. The participation of both John Monks, General Secretary of the TUC and Howard Davies, then Director General of the CBI, as well as other worthies, gave the false impression that the 'great and the good' agreed about the basic facts. It also made a number of uncontroversial policy recommendations—such as improved training—but the inclusion of unexceptional recommendations gave still further credibility to the alarmist headlines encouraged by the Joseph Rowntree Foundation's official press release. The headline read: 'Widening inequality denies millions a stake in future prosperity, warns Inquiry'. Both Howard Davies and John Monks are then quoted. Howard Davies makes a perfectly reasonable remark about preparation for global competition, but it is juxtaposed with John Monks' false claim that: 'Everyone knows the rich are getting richer and the poor are getting poorer'. The chairman's introduction to the report helps to explain the exaggerated tone of the press release. He concedes that the inquiry had a political purpose, namely to stimulate change. They would not be content with 'changing one or two rules', he said. They wanted to put their concerns 'at the top of the policy agenda'.

The HBAI method of measuring poverty has been subject to strong criticism, not only by critics of egalitarianism but also by scholars in good standing in the world of poverty research.

Professor Tony Atkinson, for example, argues that modern evidence is 'purely statistical' and lacks the qualitative information contained in the earlier local studies pioneered by Rowntree and Booth and developed by Bowley and others. According to Professor Atkinson, the strength of some earlier investigations was that researchers had conducted local surveys and spoken directly to the people being studied:

> One of the contributions of early investigators was that they were actively involved in fieldwork and that a great deal of qualitative and background material entered into their assessment. In particular, they knew a great deal about the localities they studied. When Rowntree reported the percentage in poverty in York and Bowley that in Reading, their results were given credence in part because of the local and background knowledge they brought to bear. Moreover, it was one of the insights of such investigators that the individual family or household should not be seen as an independent observation unrelated to their neighbours or work-mates.[17]

Rowntree had studied 16,000 households in his 1936 study of York and when Tout studied Bristol in 1937 he examined a 1-in-20 sample, some 4,500 households.[18] The Family Expenditure Survey, however, is a national 1-in-3,000 sample of about 7,000 to 7,500 households in the whole country. Its primary purpose is not the measurement of poverty, but to calculate the weights in the Retail Price Index. The analysts who draw conclusions from it have neither local knowledge nor the advantage of having conducted any interviews.

This tendency to study the poor as anonymous survey respondents to be analysed *en masse* is not without significance, for it tends to go hand in hand with the assumption that the people

under investigation need to have things done *for* them or *to* them
by public policy makers.

The HBAI method has been subject to withering criticism by
Professor Richard Pryke in *Taking the Measure of Poverty*[19] and
Professor Jonathan Bradshaw has advanced an equally compel-
ling critique. He has gone so far as to say that the measure of
poverty 'determines the result'. The choice of measure:

> will have consequences for the proportion and structure of the
> estimated poor population and therefore the policies that should be
> pursued to reduce or eliminate poverty. In the end the choice of poverty
> measure will be determined, if not by the availability of the data, then
> by the purpose of the research.[20]

He analysed a variety of poverty measures, focusing on twelve.
He found that the proportion of the population in poverty varied
from 10 per cent to 29 per cent, depending on the measure.[21] He
then compared the overlap between the twelve measures and
found that it varied from 99 per cent to three per cent. For
example, poverty defined as 50 per cent of mean equivalent
expenditure picked up only five per cent of poverty defined as
expenditure of more than 35 per cent of income on food (a
measure similar to the US poverty line).[22]

That different measures produce very different results has long
been known to readers of the poverty literature. Bradshaw cites
several examples, including work by Hagenaars and de Vos of
Erasmus University and Stein Ringen, then of Oslo University
now at Oxford. Hagenaars and de Vos compared eight measures
of poverty in the Netherlands and found that overlap varied from
seven per cent to 98 per cent.[23] Also in the late 1980s, Stein
Ringen produced a forthright critique of the 'income' measure of
poverty:

> it is an abstract and formal statistical exercise in which little or no
> consideration is given to how people in fact live. It is shown in this
> essay that low income does not necessarily mean a low standard of
> consumption... One needs only to introduce some very simple and
> tentative information on the standard of consumption to demonstrate
> the inadequacy of relying on income information alone in the measure-
> ment of poverty.[24]

If Bradshaw and the other critics are correct in saying that the
choice of measure determines the result, then poverty researchers should be careful to explain why a particular method was

favoured over others. Moreover, as Richard Pryke argued, the government should have been far more cautious in giving its seal of approval to a measure that is open to such strong objections. But leaving aside the limitations inherent in the FES and the HBAI series, the sound information they do provide has also been put to questionable use. If we examine more closely the two most common headline claims allegedly based on the FES—the 'poor have been getting poorer' and 'more people are below the poverty line'—they crumble when set against the actual findings.

The Poor Have Been Getting Poorer

According to a report by the Child Poverty Action Group (CPAG), since 1979 the living standards of the poor and rich have 'marched in opposite directions'. *Poverty: The Facts* claims that, between 1979 and 1992/93, the real incomes (after deducting housing costs) of those in the poorest tenth fell by 18 per cent; the average rose by 37 per cent, while the richest enjoyed a staggering rise of 61 per cent.[25]

The Joseph Rowntree Inquiry of 1995 made a similar claim. It asserted that between 1979 and 1992 the lowest income groups did not benefit from economic growth.[26] Between 1961 and 1979 average income for the whole population had risen by 35 per cent, before the deduction of housing costs (BHC), or by 33 per cent, after deducting housing costs (AHC). All income groups had benefited from this overall rise in living standards.[27] However, between 1979 and 1991/92, for the whole population, incomes grew by 36 per cent (both before and after deducting housing costs), faster than over the previous 18 years. But the growth was smaller for the bottom seven-tenths of the distribution. Moreover:

Right at the bottom, BHC incomes were no higher in 1991/92 than they had been in 1979; AHC incomes had fallen by 17 per cent.[28]

There is, the Rowntree Inquiry admits, some doubt about whether the very low incomes reported by some self-employed households are reliable, but it points out that, even excluding the self-employed: 'incomes for the poorest tenth were the same in 1991-92 as in 1979 (BHC), or were nine per cent lower than in 1979 (AHC)'. Regardless of the precise figures, it continues, the overall implication is clear:

over the period 1979 to 1992 the poorest 20-30 per cent of the population failed to benefit from economic growth, in contrast to the rest of the post-war period, when all income groups benefited during times of rising living standards.[29]

There was 'no sign of trickle-down'.[30] The tide did not raise all boats.

Consider the claim that 'the poor got poorer' between 1979 and 1992. As the above figures show, this claim is only possible if income is measured *after deduction of housing costs*. If housing costs are included then the Rowntree Inquiry found that the poorest tenth enjoyed the same income in 1992 as it had in 1979. Is it reasonable to exclude the cost of housing from a measure of the standard of living when, plainly, the home we live in is an important element in our standard of life?

The Rowntree Inquiry was based on incomes up to 1992. If we take the latest figures and compare 1979 with 1995 *after deducting housing costs*, the bottom tenth were 8 per cent worse off, but if housing costs are *not* deducted the bottom decile were ten per cent *better* off.[31]

The Rowntree Inquiry defends its use of the AHC measure because, during the 1980s, general subsidies to rents were being withdrawn and housing benefit was being increased to compensate. Thus, the average cash income of the bottom tenth (because cash income includes housing benefit) apparently increased, but there was no corresponding improvement in the standard of living.[32] The use of the AHC measure, argues the Rowntree Inquiry, removes this effect. The Rowntree Inquiry puts it like this. It says that BHC income is the best measure of the 'level' of inequality and AHC the best measure of 'trends' over time because BHC income includes higher housing benefit but 'does not correspond to any improvement in tenants' welfare'.[33]

However, the Rowntree Inquiry admits that the AHC measure suffers from a countervailing disadvantage, namely that interest payments were high during the period 1979-1992 so that deducting housing costs for mortgage holders artificially *reduces* the average income for the bottom tenth.[34]

How important is the effect of mortgage interest on the average? In fact the composition of the bottom tenth changed significantly between 1979 and 1992. In 1979 nine per cent (BHC) had been mortgage payers, whereas in 1992 the figure was 18 per cent.

The AHC measure shows 10 per cent mortgage holders in 1979 and 22 per cent in 1992.[35] Thus, the number of mortgage holders was increasing. Moreover, unusually high interest payments were being deducted from total income, artificially reducing average income on the AHC measure. Average building society interest rates varied from 11.8 per cent in 1979 to 12.7 per cent in 1991, peaking at 15.0 per cent in 1990. The highest rate in the 1960s had been 8.3 per cent in 1969 and, in the 1970s, 11.8 per cent in 1979.[36] The Rowntree Inquiry was fully aware that the AHC measure deducted interest when it was abnormally high, reflecting monetary policy rather than an increase in housing standards, but did not refrain from using the AHC measure.

To sum up: using AHC income for the bottom tenth removes housing benefit from the calculation of income on the assumption that the *whole* increase in housing benefit was to compensate for the removal of general subsidies from taxes or rates as council rents rose to market levels. That is, it assumes that there was no increase in housing standards. However, housing standards *were rising* over that period, as the edition of the HBAI report used by the Rowntree Inquiry shows. In 1979, 39 per cent of the bottom tenth (on the BHC measure) had central heating. In 1992 the proportion was 74 per cent. On the AHC measure, 42 per cent had central heating in 1979 and 77 per cent in 1992.[37]

The false assumption that housing standards did not rise and the neglect of the distorting impact of interest rates alone render the use of AHC figures indefensible. But in the appendix to his second volume, John Hills, the main researcher advising the Rowntree Inquiry, makes another admission. He states, not only that current income is best measured *before* deducting housing costs, but that an estimate of the value of home ownership and rent subsidies should be *added* to the BHC figure.[38] It will be more convenient to deal with this issue below, along with other benefits in kind, including health and education.

Thus, basing a claim about the poor getting poorer on the lower AHC figure is highly misleading. It is difficult to know, therefore, why Hills felt justified in summarising the findings of Chapter 3 of his supporting volume as follows:

> The real incomes of those in the poorest 20-30 per cent failed to rise significantly over the 1980s—and on some measures fell for those right at the bottom.[39]

On 'some' measures? In truth, *only* on the *illegitimate* AHC measure, which is low only because the cost of rents and mortgage interest has been deducted to produce an 'income' that does not measure the standard of life being enjoyed and because improvements in housing standards were ignored.

More People are Below the Poverty Line

In 1992/93, according to the CPAG, between 13 and 14 million people—around a quarter of the population—were living 'in poverty' (defined by the CPAG as living below half average income after deduction of housing costs).[40] In 1979, however, only nine per cent of the population had been living below 50 per cent of average income after deducting housing costs.

Using the benefit level as the benchmark produces a similar result. In 1992/93, 13,680,000 people (24 per cent of the population) were living 'on or below the income support level'. In 1979, 14 per cent of the population had been living on or below the supplementary benefit level. The CPAG report insists that real hardship is involved:

> Poverty is sometimes obvious—whether it is the poverty of beggars in the street, young homeless people bedded down for the night under the arches, or people rummaging in rubbish bins. At other times it is hidden inside homes, workplaces and institutions.[41]

For convenience, I will continue to concentrate my criticism on the Rowntree Inquiry of 1995, but much of the criticism applies with equal force to the Government's HBAI series on which the Rowntree Inquiry placed heavy reliance.

Since 1977, says the Rowntree Inquiry, the proportion of the population with less than half the average income has more than trebled.[42] Figure 4 of the report is used to show the main trends, which are summarised as follows:

> during the 1960s roughly 10 per cent had incomes below half the national average. After 1972 the percentage fell back to reach a low point of 6 per cent in 1977. Since then, it has risen rapidly, reaching over one in five of the population by 1990.

These figures, said the report, were before allowing for housing costs, but if housing costs are deducted, 'the equivalent rise is from 7 to 24 per cent'. Worse still, it says, 'even relative to a fixed *absolute* threshold' (50 per cent of 1979 average income after deducting housing costs), 'the proportion of the population falling below it rose from nine per cent in 1979 to 11 per cent in 1991/92'.[43]

Thus, using the moving 50 per cent threshold in its Figure 4 the report claims that (BHC) the change was from 10 per cent of the population below the 'poverty line' in 1961, via a low of six per cent in 1977, to over 20 per cent in 1991.[44] The 1979 figure was eight per cent.[45]

The comparison made against a fixed threshold (50 per cent of the 1979 average income), which the Rowntree Inquiry took direct from the *Households Below Average Income* report, showed that the percentage below the 'poverty line' moved from nine per cent in 1979 to 1ï per cent in 1991/92 (AHC). The reference given for these 'absolute' figures is Table E1 (AHC) in *Households Below Average Income* 1979-1991/92. The Rowntree Inquiry did not quote the BHC figure from the previous page of the same *Households Below Average Income* report, which shows a *fall* from eight per cent of the population below the same absolute 'poverty line' in 1979 (50 per cent of the average in 1979) to seven per cent in 1991/92.[46]

We do not know their motives for missing out the BHC figure, but we do know the result. It allowed the Rowntree Inquiry to claim that there were *more* people below the poverty line, whether the comparison is made against a moving average or a fixed threshold. However, if they had used the BHC figure throughout, they would have had to conclude that there were *fewer* people below the poverty line. The awkward BHC figure did not fit their case.[47]

Their omission of this BHC figure is particularly indefensible. Figure 4 of the report was chosen as the main illustration for their claim. It uses BHC figures. To be consistent, the text should have used a single measure throughout. Since Figure 4 uses the BHC figure, the text should also have been based on BHC income. Instead, the text sometimes used the BHC figure and sometimes the AHC. The result was a mis-statement of some of the facts. In particular, the Inquiry's main conclusion—that more people were in poverty—was not valid.

The latest figures from *Households Below Average Income* show that in 1994/95 five per cent of the population (BHC) were below 50 per cent of 1979 average income.[48]

Income Versus Expenditure

So far I have dealt with the use of the *Households Below Average Income* figures as they stand. But there is a more serious defect, namely the use of income rather than expenditure to measure the standard of living. It is widely known that the preferred measure of poverty throughout Europe is household *expenditure* not income. Initially it sounds odd that measures of expenditure and income could produce radically different results, but it has been the consistent finding of surveys conducted since the 1950s throughout Europe.

The importance of the expenditure measure has been vividly demonstrated by the Institute for Fiscal Studies (IFS), which found that the bottom 10 per cent (according to income) in 1992 spent on average 27 per cent more than in 1979 before deduction of housing costs, a finding it describes as 'startling'.[49] The latest figure, for 1995, was 28 per cent.[50]

A table in the 1997 edition of *Households Below Average Income* (covering 1979-1994/95) shows just how much variation there is between income and expenditure. Three per cent of those in the *bottom* decile for income were in the *highest* decile for expenditure, and 19 per cent were in the top 50 per cent.[51] The ownership of durable goods gives further insight into the standard of life being experienced by the bottom tenth. In 1995, 75 per cent owned a video, 85 per cent a freezer or fridge-freezer and 53 per cent had the use of a car or van.[52]

The IFS examined the possibility that the difference between income and expenditure was the result of increased debt, but found it not to be the reason. Apart from the obvious explanation that some income was not reported, a major factor was the movement of households in and out of the bottom income decile from year to year, with the effect that, in any one year, the households in the bottom tenth had savings on which they could draw.

The importance of movement in and out of the low-earning group is confirmed by the British Household Panel Survey (BHPS) which seeks to avoid one of the main defects of the HBAI approach, namely its reliance on a 'snapshot' drawn from the FES each year. The 7,000 households surveyed each year are not the same individuals and so researchers are unable to understand how particular individuals have fared over a period of time.

The BHPS seeks to overcome this problem by tracking the same
individuals. Work began in 1991 when about 5,500 households
agreed to take part in the survey. The results of the first three
interviews in 1991, 1992 and 1993 had been reported on at the
time of writing. Between 1991 and 1992, 39 per cent of the
individuals who began in the bottom income quintile had reached
a higher quintile. One year later in 1993, of those who remained
in the bottom quintile, 29 per cent had escaped to a higher
quintile and, of those who had moved out by 1992, 27 per cent
had moved back. The net result after two years was that 46 per
cent of those in the bottom quintile in 1991 were not there in
1993. (There were 2,167 individuals in the bottom quintile in
1991 and two years later 995 of them had moved out.)[53] A further
study by Amanda Gosling and colleagues at the IFS (supported
by the Joseph Rowntree Foundation) takes the analysis one year
on to 1994. Unfortunately it is based on quartiles rather than
quintiles. It also presents separate findings for men and women.
The study found that only 52 per cent of men who were in the
bottom quartile of the wage distribution in 1991 were still there
in 1994; and that only 44 per cent of the women in the bottom
earnings quartile in 1991 remained there in 1994.[54]

   Although the IFS authors found the results of the comparison
between income and expenditure 'startling' they should not have
done so, for it was consistent with all previous work. The
Statistical Office of the European Communities (Eurostat)
published a comparative study of poverty in Europe in 1990,
covering the period 1980-1985. The report states that the choice
of income or expenditure is 'particularly important' because of
under-reporting of income. When income is under-estimated it
leads to over-estimation of the incidence of poverty. As a result
of these difficulties, and after due allowance for the defects that
attend the expenditure measure, it decided to use household
expenditure because it 'better reflects the availability of both
declared and undeclared resources of low-income groups' and is
a 'more satisfactory' indicator of 'permanent income' than income
declared at some point in time.[55] The follow-up study, covering
the period up to 1988, also preferred expenditure to income.[56]

   The British poverty lobby is fully aware that the expenditure
measure is frequently preferred overseas, but disregards it. But,
they not only neglect overseas experience, they also fail to take

into account earlier British studies. The very first British study to use the Family Expenditure Survey also encountered the problem of the income/expenditure mismatch.

Abel-Smith and Townsend pioneered the use of the FES and published their findings in *The Poor and the Poorest* in 1965. They found that the 'expenditure' data for 1953/54 gave 'the more reliable indication of normal level of living', whereas by 1960 the income data from the FES were more reliable. Ideally, they would have compared both income and expenditure in 1960 with the equivalents in 1953/54 but the expenditure totals were not calculated for 1960.[57] Having been forced to compare expenditure in 1953/54 with income in 1960, they studied a sample of respondents from the 1960 survey to establish whether comparison of income and expenditure would invalidate their findings. Expenditure data for 152 households from the 1960 survey were compared with 1953/54. In addition, the Ministry of Labour studied a further 60 households. Abel-Smith and Townsend found the result 'puzzling' and concluded that it raised a number of questions about the relationship between income and expenditure which have 'serious implications for an understanding of the extent and meaning of poverty'.[58]

They also compared gross income and gross expenditure from the 1963 FES and found that the discrepancy was highest for those with the lowest declared income.[59] The average gross expenditure was 167 per cent of income for the lowest income group,[60] a discrepancy so large that they thought it justified a special inquiry.[61] Again, this result was consistent with earlier evidence from the 1953/54 FES, which had found that 10 per cent of those on national assistance reported expenditures more than twice the basic national assistance scale.[62]

Social scientists, said Abel-Smith and Townsend (in 1965), had been aware for 'many years' that in household income and expenditure surveys average expenditure 'substantially exceeds income'.[63] They gave the example of a study by Cole and Utting which had discussed the problem in 1956 and concluded that expenditure was over-stated by five per cent and income under-stated by 10 per cent.[64]

The importance of the distinction between income and expenditure has also been acknowledged by Professor Atkinson. In a very honest discussion of modern poverty analyses published in 1989, he acknowledges that earlier scholars (including Abel-Smith and Townsend) had been careful to draw attention to the difference between income and expenditure. However, 'subsequent investigators, myself included', he says, 'adopted the income definition without typically recognising the shift in emphasis'.[65]

Yet, the headline claims made by groups such as the Rowntree Inquiry and the CPAG have not used the expenditure measure.

Cash Expenditure or Total Consumption

There is a further problem with the figures deployed by the poverty lobby. So far, I have used the term 'expenditure' to mean actual spending declared to a survey. But, as Richard Pryke[66] has cogently argued, this figure leaves out the goods and services in kind that are provided free, such as health care and education. Estimates of the value of these free goods are made by the CSO (now the Office for National Statistics) and published regularly in *Economic Trends* and *Social Trends*, but are either ignored or given little weight by the poverty lobby. Not so long ago, it was common for anti-poverty campaigners to insist on the importance of the 'social wage', and trade unions made raising the social wage one of their central demands. But precisely because the 'social wage' has led to a big increase in the quality of life for the bottom tenth, the poverty lobby is now inclined to miss it out. The CSO estimate for 1994/95 shows that the bottom 20 per cent received benefits in kind (mainly health and education) worth on average £3,610 per annum. Missing out the cash value of these benefits ignores over 47 per cent of their 'final' income.[67]

Eurostat is also aware that surveys of expenditure do not take into account goods and services provided free, such as education, health care, the use of the home and durable goods. Some member states use the 'expenditure concept', (that is goods and services paid for), but the majority use the 'consumption concept' which takes into account, not only consumption for which the household pays, but free goods and services.[68]

Abel-Smith and Townsend also urged use of a wider definition of income, including capital appreciation because it was 'a major source, if not *the* major source, of the wealth of the rich'. They also called for the measurement of benefits in kind, or 'fringe benefits'.[69] They did so because their intention was to understand the true condition of the rich as well as that of the poor.

In his later work Townsend repeated his view that some families live 'very differently from what their net disposable incomes would appear to denote'. This was because:

> their command over other types of resource, whether assets, or employers' welfare, social service or private benefits in kind, is exceptional. For considerable sections of the population resources other than cash incomes form a significant part of living standards.[70]

The Rowntree Inquiry does make use of estimates of 'wealth', defined as 'marketable wealth'.[71] Indeed, the wealth figures are highlighted in the summary at the front of the report. But the report did not highlight the value of goods and services in kind.

John Hills, the main expert on whom the Rowntree Inquiry relied, was fully aware of the differences between income, cash expenditure, and the consumption measure of the standard of living. He had, for example, written about the consumption measure before working on the Rowntree Inquiry. In the second volume of the Rowntree Inquiry report he cites the CSO series which estimates the value of benefits in kind and he goes on to reproduce data from it to show how taxes and benefits affect income.[72]

Moreover, a section of his appendix (to volume 2 of the report) is devoted to the question, 'is the picture reliable?' It concedes that among the defects of the *Households Below Average Income* series is its reliance on 'cash income', excluding capital gains and benefits in kind.[73] Hills asserts that:

> other things contribute to people's standard of living. Owner-occupiers benefit from living in their home without having to pay rent. Others live rent-free or pay below-market rents.

In all these cases, he continues, adding an estimate of housing income would give a 'better measure of living standards'.[74] Housing 'income' (that is, imputed income) as a percentage of cash income is greatest for outright owners and least for local authority tenants (housing benefit is counted as part of their cash income). It is particularly significant for those on low incomes:

> Adding in housing income has a greater proportionate effect on the incomes of the poor than of the rich, and so gives a more equal income distribution than of cash incomes: 17.1 per cent of individuals had

cash incomes below half the average in 1989 according to this analysis, falling to 15.7 per cent when housing income was added.[75]

He then makes the contrast to which I have already referred above, between *current* income and the *trend* in income over time. *Current* income is best measured, not only before deducting housing costs (including rent and mortgage interest payments), but after *adding* an estimate of rent subsidies and the value of home ownership. Deducting housing costs (the AHC measure) 'produces a less equal distribution than the BHC picture' compared to the 'preferable adjustment of adding housing income'. However, he says, *trends* in AHC incomes:

> sometimes give a better guide than BHC incomes, in particular when general subsidies to tenants are withdrawn, causing both rents and Housing Benefit to rise.[76]

As we have seen above, it is not correct to attribute the whole of the difference between AHC and BHC income to the withdrawal of rent subsidies.

Later in his second volume, Hills again concedes that missing out benefits in kind has major implications for the poorest tenth. For them, average benefits from education and the NHS alone are 70 per cent of disposable (cash) income and five per cent for the richest tenth: 'Adding these in would give a much more equal distribution'.[77]

In *The Future of Welfare*, also written for the Joseph Rowntree Foundation, Hills again examines the impact of benefits in kind. They tend to equalise incomes.[78] Moreover, in other publications, Hills has tried to improve on the methods used by the CSO to arrive at estimates of income in kind, largely by supplementing the FES with information from the General Household Survey.[79]

Among the changes Hills and colleagues proposed was the re-apportionment of benefits in kind, especially to allow for the cost of students in higher education who stay away from home. The CSO treats students as separate households, since that is what they are. Hills and colleagues attribute the value of higher education to the family of origin and, as a result, found overall that people on middle incomes received the greatest gain from benefits in kind. Taking housing, education and health, they found that in total they are most valuable for the middle quintile group (£1,700), and least for the top (£1,460).[80]

However, even after their adjustments, benefits in kind are equivalent to 73 per cent of the post-tax income of the poorest fifth, compared with seven per cent for the richest fifth.[81] And they are equivalent to 42 per cent of 'final' income for bottom fifth and six per cent for the top quintile.[82]

Despite the weight of the evidence in favour of the expenditure and consumption measures, some of which was drawn to their attention by John Hills, the Rowntree Inquiry relied on cash incomes. Given that the majority of European countries use the consumption measure, that the defects of income compared with expenditure have been well known since the 1950s, and that John Hills was in the thick of efforts to refine the consumption measure, the Rowntree Inquiry's use of cash income was wholly indefensible.

3

Independence, Character and Social Policy

The tradition of thought which emphasises character and independence has a long history, and was the dominant view from about the 1830s until the First World War. It came under sharp attack at about the turn of the century and has subsequently been the subject of much caricature.

Let me begin with the characteristic view of social-policy analysts since the 1960s. They often focus on the work of the Charity Organisation Society (COS), which is widely accepted as epitomising the late-Victorian age. In re-appraising criticism of the COS we are fortunate that there has recently been a substantial increase of scholarly interest in it.[1]

The Caricature

The US historian, Bentley Gilbert, advanced a typical 1960s' line of criticism when he accused the COS of opposing all forms of public support that did not 'distinguish between the deserving and the undeserving poor, those who could be redeemed and those who could not, the elect and the damned'.[2]

Andrew Vincent and Raymond (now Lord) Plant were among the first modern scholars to re-appraise the COS. They noted that the views attributed to its spokesmen were very different from those they actually expressed. Indeed, Vincent and Plant found themselves repelled by the attitude of critics of the COS: 'The phrases about Victorian attitudes, outdated social theories and reactionary individualism', they said, pointed more to a 'polemical or ideological defensiveness' rather than 'a genuine attempt to understand the historical situation and theory of the COS'.[3] The more honest of the social-policy analysts, such as T.H. Marshall, admitted that they found it difficult to assess the COS fairly. Their philosophy, said Marshall, was 'repugnant to the modern

31

mind' and yet while the COS was 'reactionary' on some issues it had been a pioneer on others.[4]

Vincent and Plant found that the COS made no 'rigid distinction' between deserving and undeserving. Bernard Bosanquet, a leading light in the COS, had said that the words deserving and undeserving were used by the COS up to the late 1870s but that before 1893, the words were 'largely passing out of use'.[5] He was referring to a conference paper produced by his wife, Helen Bosanquet (the district secretary of the Shoreditch COS), in which she wrote:

> We will cease, therefore, to constitute ourselves arbiters of who is and who is not deserving of help. We will not use our charity as a reward of merit; if we do, we shall only foster hypocrisy and deceit; but then neither will we scatter it broadcast over good and evil alike in the vain hope that some of it will do no harm. We will rather set ourselves patiently and laboriously to understand clearly the cause of the mischief we wish to cure.[6]

The historian, Asa Briggs, accused the COS of blanket hostility to statistical measures of poverty. Vincent and Plant, however, found it 'peculiar' that Briggs should make such a claim given that C.S. Loch, the COS secretary, was the Tooke Professor of Economic Science and Statistics at King's College, London (1904-08), a member of the International Statistical Institute, and recipient of the Royal Statistical Society's Guy Medal.[7] They assume that Briggs was referring to Helen Bosanquet's objections to Seebohm Rowntree's analysis of poverty in York. She had questioned his method of measuring income, which missed out earnings by other family members and used occupational averages rather than actual incomes.[8] Vincent and Plant conclude that her criticisms of his method of data collection, as well as the validity of his dietary assumptions, 'seem perfectly valid' in the light of subsequent scholarship.[9] Jane Lewis, another of the more recent scholars to re-appraise the COS, makes a similar observation about Helen Bosanquet's criticisms of Charles Booth's study of poverty in East London.[10]

As for the COS dislike of government interference and social legislation, Vincent and Plant suggest bearing in mind 'what they actually said'.[11] They quote C.S. Loch's 1910 book, *Charity and Social Life*, in which he argued that charity would 'intensify the spirit and feeling of membership in society, and would aim at improving social conditions'. Consequently, he said, it had 'initiated many movements afterwards taken up by public authorities—such as prison reform, industrial schools, child protection, housing, food reform, etc.'[12] Vincent and Plant concluded that it was 'a misapprehension to class the Bosanquets and Loch as simple anti-government theorists or as utterly opposed to social legislation'.[13]

C.L. Mowat, in a study published in the early 1960s, claimed that the COS represented a 'sternly individualist philosophy'.[14] In fact, the Bosanquets were severe critics of 'extreme' or 'atomistic' individualism. Bernard Bosanquet argued in a paper presented to the Fabian Society in 1910 that economic individualism 'does presuppose the social organism' and that without it there would be 'a dissolution of society'. He continued:

> The Economic Individualist, indeed, who thinks the State to be unconcerned with morality, and to be unjustified in any interference on moral grounds, is a fanatic and doctrinaire, and is the precise counterpart of the Economic Socialist who assumes straight away that collectivism in property naturally implies socialisation of the will.[15]

Why did the COS emphasise character? Were they obsessed with blame? On the contrary, it was because of their belief that, whilst outsiders could give cash help, the restoration of morale and improvements in the quality of life could only come with the willing co-operation of the person being helped. Another modern scholar who has taken pains to avoid caricature, Oxford University's Jane Lewis, argues that Helen Bosanquet's whole thrust was to help people make the most of their capacities by acquiring a plan of life.[16] Mere doles weakened their resolve and encouraged acceptance of lower standards. Raising their horizons and introducing new interests in life, not designing new administrative machinery, was the key to success.[17]

The 1909 Royal Commission on the Poor Laws

I will take the proposals of the Majority of the 1909 Royal Commission on the Poor Laws (RCPL) as representative of COS thinking, not least because we have the advantage of the voluminous evidence on which members based their arguments, as well as numerous essays and books in which they described their underlying philosophy.

Today's image of the poor law is that it was too harsh; but at the turn of the century, many overseas observers thought it too lax. New Zealand and Australia, for example, refused to introduce a poor law system or any entitlement to benefit from the state, deliberately to avoid corrupting their people.[18] New Zealand parliaments, and those in some Australian states, often debated the issue but regularly rejected the introduction of a right to benefit. For them, what distinguished the British system compared with overseas schemes was not its harshness but its tradition of entitlement.

How did supporters of the Majority Report of the 1909 Royal Commission on the Poor Laws (RCPL) defend themselves? The RCPL sat from 1905 to 1909 and the COS was a major force behind the Majority Report, whose main author was Helen Bosanquet. The report, according to C.S. Loch who was also a member of the Royal Commission, was based on two central principles. The first was that by combining state financial support with practical help and guidance by voluntary organisations, a humane minimum could be maintained without increasing dependency. The second was that there was much room for the introduction of preventive measures, such as unemployment insurance. Here I will focus on the Royal Commission's proposal to divide responsibility between the state and the voluntary sector.

The Majority Report recommended the abolition of the general workhouse and that separate provision of residential relief should be made for different types of need, including children, the aged or infirm, the sick and the able-bodied. It also proposed that the Boards of Guardians be replaced in each county or county borough by a Public Assistance Authority (PAA) which would exercise overall supervision of relief. The actual work of dealing with applications and providing help would be dealt with by Public Assistance Committees whose areas would initially coincide with the former poor law unions.

In the area of each Public Assistance Authority a further two organisations were to be established. First, there would be a Voluntary Aid Council, consisting of representatives of charities, the PAA, friendly societies, trade unions, the clergy and others. In turn, it would form Voluntary Aid Committees, which would aid people in distress referred to them by the Public Assistance Committees.

The Public Assistance Committees were to be responsible for administering benefit, but a vital part of their work was to be delegated to Voluntary Aid Committees. At the heart of the work of the Voluntary Aid Committees was to be the voluntary worker or friendly visitor, who would visit, assess and offer practical help as well as moral and prudential guidance. It was intended that the Voluntary Aid Committees would attempt first to strengthen family ties and local bonds by encouraging family and friends to give support.

Thus, the intention was to maintain the centuries-old tradition of a duty on government to provide a minimum benefit, whilst avoiding the corruption of morals that had been the bane of earlier schemes. They took the view that the chief defect of a dole or entitlement was its anonymity, which was to be avoided by combining cash support with face-to-face assistance.

Underlying Philosophy

Helen Bosanquet also wrote several articles and a book defending the Majority Report.[19] In the book she describes her underlying philosophy.[20] In every country there were people who, for one reason or another, were without the necessities of life. In England, the legal responsibility for self-support lay in the first place upon each individual, if capable; in the second upon the family; and failing both upon the taxpayers.[21] Helen Bosanquet upheld the principle of a public duty to help:

> no greater blow could be struck at the feeling of unity which holds a community together than that a part of it should be allowed to perish for want while another part could have assisted and did not.[22]

But to say as much was just the start: 'a community owes much more to its members than the mere maintenance of life; and it is by aiming so low that it achieves such deplorable results'.[23] True respect should involve making demands. We cannot grow as people without a struggle to overcome difficulties. Consequently, thoughtless help, she said, could make matters worse. In particular, some people neglect relationships that would allow them to ask for help in a spirit of mutual respect: they allow friendships to wither, or neglect family ties, or do not join organisations that would lend a helping hand.

Hostility to Deterrence

The practical problem for reformers was that the mere fact that provision existed for those who failed in their 'primary duty' of self-support caused 'many to fail who might otherwise have succeeded'.[24] The problem of public assistance was, therefore, to offer help, 'in such a way as to diminish rather than to increase the number of those requiring it'.[25] Two approaches were available:

> the one to make the conditions of assistance so disagreeable that no one will accept them who can possibly help it; the other to make the assistance so effective that it will ultimately remove the cause of distress.[26]

She did not favour a policy of simple deterrence, but rather supported the second approach. The true test of good adminis-tration was:

> the degree of success which it achieves in combining a policy which shall not encourage laziness and self-indulgence with one which shall be really remedial in the assistance afforded. It fails when it is attractive to the profligate, but it fails no less when it is deterrent to those who might be restored by its services to health and independ-ence.[27]

The poor law as it stood in 1909 was not succeeding in this task, and the most serious failure had been in dealing with the able-bodied. The policy of the authorities had aimed at deter-rence, but it had 'failed conspicuously to deter the idle and worthless who are indifferent to humiliation so long as they are well-fed'.[28] She emphasised the diversity of those who needed assistance:

> The population which comes within the scope of the Poor Law is made up of the most heterogeneous elements. Individuals of every age, of every shade of character, of every degree of physical or moral incapac-ity, with every variety of disease or disability, are all brought together by the one common fact that they demand to be maintained at the cost of the community.[29]

No society can simply pay anyone who asks—and so someone must decide whether or not to assist and what form the assis-tance should take.

In her earlier book, *The Strength of the People*, she criticised the new tendency to treat those below the 'poverty line' as incapable of self-support. We 'manufacture' our poor by 'our crude belief that the Poverty Line is a question of money, and that by merely putting money or money's worth into a man's hands we can raise him above it' and by our 'ignorant meddling which robs human lives of far more than we give in return'.[30]

Should we, therefore, do nothing? Should we 'stand by and never lend a hand to our brother in his difficulties?' Is there no way by which 'the strong can help the weak, the rich help the poor?' She continues:

> The strong can help the weak, there is no doubt about that; they may even help the poor to be less poor; but money will play a very subordinate part in their work.[31]

The economic position of any individual, or group of individuals, is, she argues, so dependent upon 'qualities which are not primarily or obviously economic' that we will only discover the best method of improving the economic position of the people if we enlist 'the whole mind and interests of the people in question'.[32]

The Majority Report did not maintain that deficiencies of character were always and necessarily the problem: 'There are some who are physically or morally incapable of independence under any administration; and there are many who are not to be tempted from it by anything less than sheer necessity.'[33] However, there were also many people who:

> simply follow the line of least resistance, who are quite capable of earning their living, and will do so in the absence of any temptation to the contrary, but who are easily drawn into loafing and thriftlessness by the prospect of relief. It is to these people on the borderland that an unwise policy of relief on easy terms is fatal; they quickly lose the habits of energy and foresight, and become in the true sense of the word pauperised.[34]

Mrs Bosanquet accepted that:

> in specially selected cases of men thrown out of work by unexpected misfortune, the wisest as well as the kindest form of help may be to give an allowance whilst they seek new work. But it is a form of help which is most wisely given privately, out of charitable funds. When given wholesale from public funds there is no form of relief which may so quickly demoralise a neighbourhood.[35]

Character

I will focus a little more on 'character', a key term for the COS which, since the 1960s, has been likely to occasion ridicule. As Cambridge scholar Stefan Collini has remarked, mention of the term 'character' today may be interpreted as a tactic intended to impose middle-class values on the working class. But this assumption, he said, is not consistent with the fact that late-Victorian socialists also advocated good character.[36]

According to Collini, character was a 'democratic' virtue closely linked to liberalism. It had been associated with a spirit of assertiveness, not least by the new working-class voters after 1867. For writers such as John Bright or Samuel Smiles, the language of character was 'a public affirmation of one's own worth in the face of a daily experience of the condescension of the well-born and well-connected'.[37] It especially implied a revolt against the 'artificiality', and 'outward polish' of the aristocratic 'upper-crust'. For the down-to-earth democrat, it was essential that the personal qualities of an individual should be genuine.[38] Samuel Smiles, for instance, constantly insisted that character was unrelated to social position. The true worth of a person was a separate matter.[39]

There was another element to the late-Victorian idea of character. Each should cultivate fortitude in the face of adversity. Today it is common to claim that we live in a fast-changing world driven by global competition, as if we were the first to do so. The Victorians, however, had the same sense and with no less justification. According to Collini:

> Victorian intellectuals were self-consciously members of a society in the van of progress: the first arrivals in the future cannot be sure what to expect, and no particular technical expertise can be guaranteed in advance to be relevant.[40]

Consequently, it was best to rely, not so much on 'training' in any particular skill or expertise, but on more general virtues, such as courage, adaptability and endurance. As Collini noted, 'character' was 'an ideal peculiarly suited to a future of unknown circumstances'.[41] The ideal Victorian possessed self-command and was ready for anything. Each was determined not to 'crack' under pressure or 'let the side down'.[42] Good character, in the sense described by Collini, remains as important today as in Victorian times.

Responsibility and Blame

The focus of the COS on personal responsibility led many to caricature its view as blaming the innocent, or 'blaming the victim' in modern parlance. According to this caricature the COS was doing no more than making excuses for neglect, because having established that all hardship was the fault of the individual, then it followed that nothing should be done to help them.

To understand its view of personal responsibility it is necessary to be aware that it derives from the philosophical tradition known as idealism. Fortunately we do not need to dive too deeply into metaphysical water to understand this approach, which both the Bosanquets took pains to explain in accessible language.

At its heart is the relationship between the individual mind and outside circumstances. They were not solipsists who thought that everything was in the mind. Nor were they extreme empiricists who thought that there was nothing but brute facts.

At one level the human mind was plainly the unique property of each individual with all its idiosyncrasies. However, the ideas contained in it—the beliefs held, the inclinations, emotions, etc.—were also at one and the same time personal and yet shared with others. For instance, habits like honesty, such that an individual is 'incapable' of telling a lie, as well as institutions like marriage or the family, are cultural endowments or inheritances which we have in common with our ancestors and like-minded contemporaries. They are not purely 'personal values'. They may have been taught deliberately, or transmitted by example. Hayek took a similar view.[43]

Critics of the COS often asserted that man is a 'social animal', as if they were contradicting the COS. But they were not. As Helen Bosanquet put it, there was a 'kind of dependence on the community':

> which is essential to the whole mental development of man. It is to his social environment that he must look for that inherited knowledge and skill which the animal inherits in its physical organism. Every human being begins again practically at the beginning: nothing is his when he enters life of the vast acquisitions made by his ancestors. But he finds it waiting for him, stored in the social community into which he is born. In its language, its institutions, its knowledge, its skill, there awaits him the inheritance prepared for him.[44]

The Bosanquets fully accepted that we are heirs to a culture which is an integral part of our personality, but this culture is not mechanically imprinted on our brains. To benefit from what civilisation bequeaths us, we must be active recipients. As Helen Bosanquet put it in *The Strength of the People*, we can enter into our inheritance 'only by way of conscious effort'. Each must 'learn and work and actively possess himself of all that he desires to partake in' before the community can 'yield his inheritance to him'.[45] Each must 'wrest its gifts from it by his own toil'.[46]

What are the implications for people who at any one time are in need of material support? Is it possible that a person could be unable to be self-supporting 'through no fault of his own'? Or is it always his own fault? A person can plainly fall on hard times through bad luck or misfortune, said the Bosanquets. However, 'circumstances' are not wholly external. They do not just happen. Circumstances are not merely 'outside forces'. Deliberately using the word in its widest sense, Helen Bosanquet argued that:

> it is always the man in his selective activity who makes his circum-
> stances, who chooses what his world shall be, even though he may let
> them afterwards mould his life by the habits they encourage.[47]

A person's choice of friends, said Helen Bosanquet, reveals character. Who does he associate with: 'Tell me who a man's friends are, and I will tell you what he is', not because they make him what he is, so much as because he has revealed himself in his choice.[48] So too does choice of neighbourhood: 'Those who live in quiet streets are those who like quiet streets; and if they do not like them, they soon change them to noisy ones.'[49] A change of circumstances will make no difference to conduct unless the change is chosen:

> Again, change in the actual material surroundings of people is not only
> useless, it cannot be made to continue, unless the people can be made
> to take an interest in them, and deliberately choose them for their
> circumstances.[50]

Of course, she accepted that a 'conscious choice' was not always made. More often, a person did not know that he was rejecting one circumstance in favour of another. Rather, he was 'simply attracted' to what interested him, and his interests depended upon what he already had in his mind. If he has no interests in the 'higher sense', she says, 'then his appetites and habits will make his circumstances'.[51]

To give a modern example, a man may lose his job in shipbuilding because the yard closes. It was not his fault. His circumstances were made for him. But if he is still there a year later waiting for 'something to turn up', he has made matters worse. He has 'chosen' his circumstances.

Conclusion

The tendency of many poverty researchers to analyse poverty as if it were the result of 'outside forces' acting on powerless individuals has had a disabling impact on efforts to overcome reliance on state benefits. As the reformers at the turn of the century argued, reliance on state welfare can only be overcome if the active enthusiasm of benefit recipients is enlisted. If they were right, we need to renew our faith in the capacity of people to overcome adversity and to devise new public policies that encourage the best in people.

Earlier reformers attributed personal responsibility to individuals, but they did not see personal responsibility as synonymous with blame. They focused on responsibility—on character—because it offered the most certain escape from poverty and dependency for most people. They did not claim that individuals were always responsible—let alone to blame—for their predicament. They knew full well that there are many events and brute facts beyond the control of any one person, or indeed of any organised community. But the human condition was to be blessed with powers of judgement and reason, and we could only lead a full life if we made use of our capacities. All should strive to make the most of their circumstances. The paramount aim in providing help to people who have fallen on hard times should be to empower them to claim their birthright of independence, not to render them content to lie down under their difficulties. As black US presidential candidate, Jesse Jackson, once said: 'If a white man knocks you down, its his fault; if you don't get up, its yours'.

Notes

Introduction

1   de Tocqueville, A., *Memoir on Pauperism*, London: IEA, 1997.

2   Royal Commission on the Poor Laws and the Relief of Distress, *Report*, London: HMSO, 1909, para. 22.

3   Kempson, E., *Life on a Low Income*, York: YPS/Joseph Rowntree Foundation, 1996, p. 169.

4   *Social Trends*, No. 27, London: HMSO, 1997, Table 8.4.

5   *Ibid.* All figures are at 1995/96 prices.

6   *Financial Times*, 1st October 1997.

7   Commission on Social Justice, *Social Justice: Strategies for National Renewal*, London: Vintage, 1994.

8   Field, F., *Making Welfare Work*, London: Institute of Community Studies, 1995.

Dependence and Independence: the Trends

1   RCPL, *Report*, p. 19.

2   Beveridge, W.H., *Social Insurance and Allied Services*, Cmnd 6404, London: HMSO, 1942, pp. 218-19.

3   *Ibid.*, pp. 211-12.

4   *Ibid.*, pp. 212-213.

5   Local Government Board, Annual Report, 1871, p. xiii; 1901, p. li. The figures for 1871 and 1901 can be compared with those from the Royal Commission on the Poor Laws of 1909, which produced calculations for England and Wales based on averages for the 8-10 year trade cycles in which each year occurred. They are based on day counts in January and July to take account of seasonal variations. Because the figures are based on the number claiming on a given day, they do not measure the number of people who had relied on the poor law at some point during a given year. See also RCPL, *Report*, 1909, p. 20.

6   1921, p. 79.

7   1931, pp. 192-3.

8 Report of the National Assistance Board, 1951, Cmnd 8632, London: HMSO, pp. 5-6; Report of the National Assistance Board, 1961, Cmnd 1730, London: HMSO, p. 14. Population estimates are from the *Annual Abstract of Statistics*, 1996.

9 1971, Cmnd 5019, London: HMSO, 1972, pp. 117, 337.

10 p. 186.

11 See also *Low Income Statistics: Households Below Average Income Tables 1988*, House of Commons, 1990-91, Social Security Committee, First Report, pp. lii-liii.

12 See also *Households Below Average Income 1979-1993/94*, HMSO, 1996, p. 123; and from *Households Below Average Income 1979-1991/92*, p. 69.

13 HBAI, 1990/91, p. 69, 1991/92 p. 69, 1992/93 p. 71, 1993/94, p. 123.

Poverty Inflation

1 Peter Townsend, for instance, assumes that participation in the accepted lifestyle can be made possible by giving cash to the 'excluded': in *Poverty in the United Kingdom*, Harmondsworth: Penguin, 1979, p. 915.

2 Dennis, N., *The Invention of Permanent Poverty*, London: IEA, 1997, Chapter 13.

3 Townsend, P., *op. cit.*, 1979.

4 *Ibid.*, p. 248.

5 *Ibid.*, p. 249.

6 *Ibid.*, pp. 249-51.

7 *Ibid.*, p. 273, pp. 301-2.

8 *Ibid.*, p. 273, pp. 301-2.

9 Rowntree, B.S., *Poverty: A Study of Town Life*, London: Macmillan, 1901; Rowntree, B.S., *Poverty and Progress*, London: Longmans, 1941; Rowntree, B.S. and Lavers, G.R., *Poverty and the Welfare State*, London: Longmans, 1951.

10 Townsend, P., *op. cit.*, p. 914.

11 Atkinson, A.B., *Poverty and Social Security*, London: Harvester Wheatsheaf, 1989, p. 49.

12 Dennis, N., *op. cit.*,1997.

13 Townsend, P., *op. cit.*, p. 337.

14 *Ibid.*, p. 916.

15 *Ibid.*, p. 893.

16 *Ibid.*, p. 926.

17 Atkinson, A.B., *op. cit.*, pp. 23-24; see also p. 38, pp. 47-48.

18 *Ibid.*, p. 43.

19 Pryke, R., *Taking the Measure of Poverty*, London: IEA, 1995.

20 Bradshaw, J., Bouwknegt, L. and Holmes, H., 'In search of a representative measure of poverty', in Smith, P. (ed.), *Measuring Outcome in the Public Sector*, London: Taylor & Francis, 1996, pp. 135-53.

21 *Ibid.*, p. 148.

22 *Ibid.*, p. 150.

23 Hagenaars, A. and de Vos, K., 'The definition and measurement of poverty', *Journal of Human Resources*, 1988, Vol. XXIII, No. 2, p. 219.

24 Ringen, S., 'Direct and indirect measures of poverty', *Journal of Social Policy*, Vol. 17, No. 2, 1988, p. 363.

25 Oppenheim, C., *Poverty: the Facts*, London: Child Poverty Action Group, 1993, p. 1.

26 *Joseph Rowntree Foundation Inquiry into Income and Wealth*, York: Joseph Rowntree Foundation, 1995, Vol. 1, p. 6.

27 *Ibid.*, p. 15.

28 There are slight differences between the CPAG and JRI figures: The CPAG claims an 18% fall; the JRI 17%; and the CPAG claims growth of 37% and the JRI 36%.

29 *Rowntree Inquiry*, Vol. 1, p. 15.

30 *Ibid.*, p. 8.

31 DSS, *Households Below Average Income: A Statistical Analysis 1979-1994/95*, London: HMSO, 1997, p. 116.

32 Hills, J., *Joseph Rowntree Foundation Inquiry into Income and Wealth*, Vol. 2, 1995, pp. 109-10.

33 *Ibid.*, p. 24.

34 *Ibid.*, p. 25.

35 HBAI, 1992/93, p. 173.

36 Goodman, A. and Webb, S., *For Richer, For Poorer: The Changing Distribution of Income in the UK, 1961-91*, London: Institute for Fiscal Studies,1994, A1.

37 HBAI, p. 139.

38 Hills, J., *op. cit.*, Vol. 2, p. 109.

39 *Ibid.*, p. 36.

40 Oppenheim, C., *op. cit.*, p. 24.

41 *Ibid.*, p. 1.

42 *Rowntree Inquiry*, Vol. 1, p. 15.

43 *Ibid.*, p. 15

44 Based on Goodman, A. and Webb, S., *op. cit.*, 1994, Fig. 2.7, A12.

45 Goodman and Webb, *op. cit.*; and HBAI, 1979-1991/92, F1(BHC).

46 HBAI, 1979-1991/92, E1(BHC).

47 *Rowntree Inquiry*, Vol. 1., p. 15.

48 DSS, *Households Below Average Income: A Statistical Analysis 1979-1994/95*, London: HMSO, 1997, p. 139.

49 Goodman, A. and Webb, S., *The Distribution of UK Household Expenditure 1979-1992*, London: Institute for Fiscal Studies, 1995, p. 25.

50 DSS, *Households Below Average Income: A Statistical Analysis 1979-1994/95*, London: HMSO, 1997, p. 89.

51 *Ibid.*, p. 93.

52 *Ibid.*, p. 110.

53 Goodman, A., Johnson, P., Webb, S., *Inequality in the UK*, London: Oxford University Press, 1997, pp. 260-61.

54 Gosling, A., Johnson, P., McCrae, J. and Paull, G., *The Dynamics of Low Pay and Unemployment in Early 1990s Britain*, London: Institute for Fiscal Studies, 1997, pp. 45-46.

55 Eurostat, *Poverty in Figures: Europe in the Early 1980s*, Luxembourg: Office for Official Publications of the European Communities, 1990.

56 Eurostat, *Poverty Statistics in the Late 1980s: Research based on micro-data*, Luxembourg: Office for Official Publications of the European Communities, 1994.

57 Abel-Smith, B., and Townsend, P., *The Poor and the Poorest*, London: Bell, 1965, pp. 21-22.

58 *Ibid.*, p. 23.

59 *Ibid.*, p. 23.

60 *Ibid.*, Table 1, p. 24.

61 *Ibid.*, p. 25.

62 *Ibid.*, p. 33.

63 *Ibid.*, p. 23.

64 *Ibid.*, p. 24.

65 Atkinson, A.B., *op. cit.*, 1989, p. 11.

66 Pryke, R. *op. cit.*, 1995.

67 CSO, *Social Trends 26*, London: HMSO, 1996, p. 107.

68 Eurostat, *op. cit.*, 1990, p. 12.

69 Abel-Smith, B. and Townsend, P., *op. cit.*, 1965, p. 10.

70 Townsend, P., *op. cit.*, 1979, p. 271.

71 *Rowntree Inquiry*, Vol. 1., p. 31.

72 Hills, J., Vol. 2, p. 16. He makes use of the *Economic Trends* series again on pages 23 and 56.

73 *Ibid.*, p. 106.

74 *Ibid.*, p. 109.

75 *Ibid.*, p. 109.

76 *Ibid.*, p. 109.

77 *Ibid.*, p. 111.

78 Hill, J., *The Future of Welfare*, York: Joseph Rowntree Foundation, 1993, Fig 9.

79 Evandrou, M., Falkingham, J., Hills, J. and Le Grand, J., *The Distribution of Welfare Benefits in Kind*, London: STICERD, 1992. For another approach see Pryke, *op. cit.*, 1995.

80 *Ibid.*, p. 19.

81 *Ibid.*, p. 7. Table 2, p. 8.

82 *Ibid.*, p. 8.

Independence, Character and Social Policy

1 For example, Lewis, J., *The Voluntary Sector, The State and Social Work in Britain*, Aldershot: Edward Edgar, 1995.

2 Gilbert, B.B., *The Evolution of National Insurance in Great Britain*, London: Michael Joseph, 1966, p. 52.

3 Vincent, A. and Plant, R., *Philosophy, Politics and Citizenship*, Oxford: Blackwell, 1984, p. 100.

4 Marshall, T.H., *Social Policy in the Twentieth Century*, 2nd edition, London: Hutchinson, 1967, p. 167. See Vincent and Plant, *op. cit.*, p. 99.

5 Bosanquet, B., *Social and International Ideals*, London: Macmillan, 1917, p. 112.

6 Dendy, H., 'The meaning and methods of true charity', in Bosanquet, B. (ed.), *Aspects of the Social Problem*, London: Macmillan, 1895, p. 172; originally published as 'Thorough Charity' by the Charity Organisation Society. (Helen Dendy became Helen Bosanquet.)

7 Vincent, A. and Plant, R., *op. cit.*, 1984, p. 98.

8 Bosanquet, H., 'The poverty line', *Charity Organisation Review*, 1903, pp. 9-23.

9 Vincent, A. and Plant, R., *op. cit.*, 1984, p. 98.

10 Lewis, J., 'Social facts, social theory and social change: the ideas of Booth in relation to those of Beatrice Webb, Octavia Hill and Helen Bosanquet', in Englander, D. and O'Day, R. (eds.), *Retrieved Riches: Social Investigation in Britain 1840-1914*, Aldershot: Scolar Press, 1995, p. 62.

11 Vincent, A. and Plant, R., *op. cit.*, 1984, p. 97.

12 Loch, C.S., *Charity and Social Life*, London: Macmillan, 1910, p. 367.

13 Vincent, A. and Plant, R., *op. cit.*,1984, p. 97.

14 Mowat, C.L., *The Charity Organisation Society 1869-1913*, London: Methuen, 1961, p. 38.

15 Bosanquet, B., 'The antithesis between individualism and socialism philosophically considered', *Charity Organisation Review*, September 1890, p. 360.

16 Lewis, J., 'Social facts, social theory and social change: the ideas of Booth in relation to those of Beatrice Webb, Octavia Hill and Helen Bosanquet', 1995, p. 61.

17 *Ibid.*, p. 62.

18 Thomson, D., *The History of the Welfare State in New Zealand*, Auckland: forthcoming; Kewley, T.H., *Social Security in Australia 1900-1972*, second edition, Sydney: Sydney University Press, 1973, p. 7, note 9. South Australia was an exception.

19 Bosanquet, H., *The Poor Law Report of 1909*, London: Macmillan, 1909.

20 *Ibid.*, p. 1.

21 *Ibid*, p. 3.

22 Bosanquet, H., *The Strength of the People*, London, Macmillan, 1903, second edition, p. 110.

23 *Ibid.*, p. 110.

24 Bosanquet,H., *op. cit.*,1909, p. 4.

25 *Ibid.*, p. 5.

26 *Ibid.*, p. 5.

27 *Ibid.*, p. 6.

28 *Ibid.*, pp. 7-8.

29 *Ibid.*, pp. 8-9.

30 Bosanquet, H., *op. cit.*, 1903, p. 108.

31 *Ibid.*, p. 109.

32 *Ibid.*, p. 109.

33 Bosanquet, H., *op. cit.*, 1909, p. 39.

34 *Ibid.*, p. 39.

35 Bosanquet, H., *op. cit.*, 1903, p. 109.

36 Collini, S., *Public Moralists*, Oxford: Clarendon, 1993, p. 93.

37 *Ibid.*, p. 113.

38 *Ibid.*, p. 106.

39 Smiles, S., *Self-Help*, London: IEA, 1996.

40 Collini, S., *op. cit.*, 1993, pp. 113-14.

41 *Ibid.*, p. 113.

42 *Ibid.*, p. 116.

43 Hayek, F.A., *The Sensory Order*, London: Routledge, 1952.

44 Bosanquet, H., *op. cit.*, 1903, p. 38.

45 *Ibid.*, p. 38.

46 *Ibid.*, p. 38.

47 *Ibid.*, p. 44.

48 *Ibid.*, p. 44.

49 *Ibid.*, p. 46.

50 *Ibid.*, p. 47.

51 *Ibid.*, pp. 51-2.